Air Fryer Kitchen

Healthy and Effortless Recipes to Fry, Bake, Grill and Roast the Most Delicious Dishes at Home

Destinee Bullock

© Copyright 2021. All rights reserved.

The following Book is reproduced below with the goal of providing information that is as accurate and reliable as possible. Regardless, purchasing this Book can be seen as consent to the fact that both the publisher and the author of this book are in no way experts on the topics discussed within and that any recommendations or suggestions that are made herein are for entertainment purposes only. Professionals should be consulted as needed prior to undertaking any of the action endorsed herein.
This declaration is deemed fair and valid by both the American Bar Association and the Committee of Publishers Association and is legally binding throughout the United States.

Furthermore, the transmission, duplication, or reproduction of any of the following work including specific information will be considered an illegal act irrespective of if it is done electronically or in print. This extends to creating a secondary or tertiary copy of the work or a recorded copy and is only allowed with the express written consent from the Publisher. All additional right reserved.

The information in the following pages is broadly considered a truthful and accurate account of facts and as such, any inattention, use, or misuse of the information in question by the reader will render any resulting actions solely under their purview. There are no scenarios in which the publisher or the original author of this work can be in any fashion deemed liable for any hardship or damages that may befall them after undertaking information described herein.

Additionally, the information in the following pages is intended only for informational purposes and should thus be thought of as universal. As befitting its nature, it is presented without assurance regarding its prolonged validity or interim quality. Trademarks that are mentioned are done without written consent and can in no way be considered an endorsement from the trademark holder.

CONTENTS

BREAKFAST 1
Blackberries Cornflakes Bowl 2
Egg Paprika Scramble 3
White Mushroom Pie 4
Morning Cauliflower Bake 6
Cheese Bread Pizza 7
Cherry Tomato Omelet 8
Polenta Bites 10
Sweet Vanilla Toast 12
Farro Breakfast Risotto 13
Tapioca Pudding 15
Sweetened Breakfast Oats 17
LUNCH 19
Low Country Boil 20
Shrimp and Grits 23
Crust less Crab Quiche 26
Lemon Pepper Salmon 29
Shrimp with Tomatoes and Feta 31
Scallops And Spring Veggies 33
Air Fryer Salmon Patties 35
Salmon Noodles 37
Beer-battered fish and chips 39
Tuna Stuffed Potatoes 41
Fried Calamari 43
Soy And Ginger Shrimp 44
Crispy Cheesy Fish Fingers 46
Panko-Crusted Tilapia 48
Potato Crusted Salmon 49
Salmon Croquettes 50
Snapper Scampi 52
Thai Fish Cakes With Mango Relish 54
Air Fryer Fish Tacos 56
Firecracker shrimp 57
Sesame Seeds Coated Fish 59
DINNER 61
Turkey Breasts with Greek Mustard Sauce 62
Country-Style Nutty Turkey Breast 64

Eggs and Sausage with Keto Rolls *66*
Bacon-Wrapped Turkey with Cheese *68*
Italian-Style Spicy Chicken Breasts *70*
Classic Chicken Nuggets *72*
Thai Chicken with Bacon *74*
Thanksgiving Turkey with Mustard Gravy...................................... *76*
Pretzel Crusted Chicken With Spicy Mustard Sauce *78*
Chinese-Style Sticky Turkey Thighs... *81*
Easy Hot Chicken Drumsticks *83*
Crunchy Munchy Chicken Tenders With Peanuts *85*
Tarragon Turkey Tenderloins With Baby Potatoes........................ *87*
Mediterranean Chicken Breasts With Roasted Tomatoes............. *89*
Thai Red Duck With Candy Onion... *91*
Rustic Chicken Legs With Turnip Chips *93*
Old-Fashioned Chicken Drumettes *95*
Easy Ritzy Chicken Nuggets.. *97*
Asian Chicken Filets With Cheese *99*
Paprika Chicken Legs With Brussels Sprouts *101*
Chinese Duck *103*
Turkey Bacon With Scrambled Eggs... *105*

BREAKFAST

Blackberries Cornflakes Bowl

Prep Time 10 m | Cooking Time 10 m | 4 Servings

Ingredients:

3 cups of milk

One tablespoon sugar

Two eggs whisked

¼ tablespoon nutmeg, a ground

¼ cup blackberries

Four tablespoon cream cheese, whipped

1½ cups of corn flakes

Instructions:

1. Add everything to a suitably sized bowl and stir well. Add this prepared

mixture to the Instant Pot. Put on the Instant Air Fryer lid and cook on Air

Fryer mode for 10 minutes at 350 degrees F. Once done, remove the lid and

serve warm.

Per serving: Calories: 180 Protein: 5 Carbs: 12g Fat: 5g

Egg Paprika Scramble

Prep Time 10 m | Cooking Time 10 m | 6 Servings

Ingredients:

Four eggs whisked

A drizzle olive oil

Salt and black pepper to taste

One red onion, chopped

Two teaspoons sweet paprika

Instructions:

1. Add everything to a suitably sized bowl and stir well. Add this prepared

mixture to the Instant Pot. Put on the Instant Air Fryer lid and cook on Bake

mode for 10 minutes at 200 degrees F. Once done, remove the lid and serve

warm.

Per serving: Calories: 190 Protein: 4g Carbs: 12g Fat: 7g

White Mushroom Pie

Prep Time 10 m | Cooking Time 20 m | 6 Servings

Ingredients:

One tablespoon olive oil

9inch pie dough

Six white mushrooms, chopped

Two tablespoon bacon cooked and crumbled

Three eggs

One red onion, chopped

½ cup heavy cream

Salt and black pepper to taste

½ tablespoon thyme, a dried

¼ cup cheddar cheese, grated

Instructions:

1. Grease a pie pan with oil, suitable to fit the Instant Pot. Spread the dough in

the pie pan. Beat everything in a bowl except the cheese. Pour this mixture

over the dough and drizzle cheese on top. Put on the Instant Air Fryer lid and

cook on Bake mode for 10 minutes at 400 degrees F. Once done, remove the

lid and serve warm.

Per serving: Calories: 192 Protein: 7g Carbs: 14g Fat: 6g

Morning Cauliflower Bake

Prep Time 10 m | Cooking Time 10 m | 4 Servings

Ingredients:

One cauliflower head stems removed, florets separated and steamed

Three carrots, chopped and steamed

2 oz. cheddar cheese, grated

Three eggs

2 oz. milk

Two teaspoon cilantro, chopped

Salt and black pepper to taste

Instructions:

1. Beat eggs with salt, pepper, parsley, and milk in a bowl. Spread the carrots

and cauliflower in the Instant Pot. Pour the egg mixture over them. Put on

the Instant Air Fryer lid and cook on Bake mode for 20 minutes at 350

degrees F. Once done, remove the lid and serve warm.

Per serving: Calories: 194 Protein: 6g Carbs: 11g Fat: 4g

Cheese Bread Pizza

Prep Time 8 m | Cooking Time 14 m | 4 Servings

Ingredients:

Six bread slices

Five tablespoon butter, melted

Three garlic cloves, minced

Six teaspoon basil and tomato pesto

1 cup mozzarella cheese, grated

Instructions:

1. Spread the bread slices on the working surface. Whisk butter with garlic and

pesto in a bowl. Spread this mixture over the slices. Set the air fryer basket

in the Instant Pot and place the pizza slices in the Air fryer basket and drizzle

half of the cheese over them. Put on the Instant Air Fryer lid and cook on Air

Fry mode for 8minutes at 350 degrees F. Once done, remove the cover and

serve warm.

Per serving:

Calories: 187 Protein: 5 g Carbs: 13g Fat: 6g

Cherry Tomato Omelet

Prep Time 11 m | Cooking Time 15 m | 4 Servings

Ingredients:

One sausage link, sliced

Two eggs whisked

Four cherry tomatoes halved

One tablespoon cilantro, chopped

One tablespoon olive oil

One tablespoon cheddar cheese, grated

Salt and black pepper to taste

Instructions:

1. Add sausage and tomatoes to the Instant Pot. Put on the Instant Air Fryer lid

and cook on Bake mode for 5 minutes at 350 degrees F. Once done, remove

the cover and serve warm. Take a pan, suitable to fit the Instant Pot. Add the

sausage and tomatoes to the pan. Whisk remaining things in a bowl and pour

it over the vegetables. Place this pan in the Instant pot and put on the Instant

Air Fryer lid and cook on Bake mode for 6minutes at 360 degrees F. Once

done, remove the lid and serve warm.

Per serving:

Calories: 270 Protein: 16g Carbs: 23g Fat: 14g

Polenta Bites

Prep Time 10 m | Cooking Time 15 m | 4 Servings

Ingredients:

1 cup cornmeal

3 cups of water

Salt and black pepper to taste

One tablespoon butter softened

¼ cup potato starch

A drizzle vegetable oil

Maple syrup for serving

Instructions:

1. Add water and cornmeal to a pot and cook for 10 minutes on medium heat.

Stir in butter and mix well, then put off the heat. Once the cornmeal is

cooled, make small balls out of it. Place them in a greased baking pan and

flatten them with a press of your hand. Drizzle oil over them then places the

container in the Instant Pot. Put on the Instant Air Fryer lid and cook on

Bake mode for 15 minutes at 380 degrees F. Once done, remove the cover

and allow the bites to cool. Garnish with maple syrup and serve.

Per serving:

Calories: 170 Protein: 4g Carbs: 12g Fat: 2g

Sweet Vanilla Toast

Prep Time 5 m | Cooking Time 10 m | 6 Servings

Ingredients:

One stick butter softened

12 bread slices

½ cup brown sugar

Two teaspoon vanilla extract

Instructions:

1. Beat butter with vanilla and sugar in a bowl. Place the bread slices on the

working surface and spread the butter mixture over them. Place all the

slices in the Air fryer basket inside the Instant Pot. Put on the Instant Air

Fryer lid and cook on Air Fry mode for 5 minutes at 400 degrees F. Once

done, remove the lid and serve fresh.

Per serving:

Calories: 170 Protein: 2g Carbs: 11g Fat: 6g

Farro Breakfast Risotto

Prep Time 10 m | Cooking Time 12 m | 4 Servings

Ingredients:

1 cup farro

1 tsp Italian seasoning

1/2 cup parmesan cheese, grated

1/2 cup mozzarella cheese, grated

2 tbsp. heavy whipping cream

2 cups vegetable stock

1 tbsp. butter

Instructions:

1. Add butter into the instant pot and set the pot on sauté mode.

2. Add farro and cook for 2 minutes. Add stock and stir everything well.

3. Seal pot with lid and cook on manual high pressure for 10 minutes.

4. Once done then allow to release pressure naturally for 10 minutes then

release using the quick-release method. Open the lid.

5. Add remaining ingredients and stir well.

6. Serve and enjoy.

Per serving:

Calories 206 Fat 13.7 g Carbohydrates 13.4 g Sugar 1.8 g Protein

9.9 g Cholesterol 37 mg

Tapioca Pudding

Prep Time 10 m | Cooking Time 7 m | 4 Servings

Ingredients:

1/2 cup tapioca

2 cups of water

2 egg yolks

1/2 tsp vanilla

1/2 cup sugar

1/2 cup milk

Instructions:

1. Add water and tapioca into the instant pot and stir well.

2. Seal pot with lid and cook on high pressure for 5 minutes.

3. Once done then release pressure using the quick-release method than open

the lid.

4. Set pot on sauté mode. In a small bowl, whisk together milk and egg yolks

5. Slowly pour egg mixture into the pot and stir constantly.

6. Add vanilla and sugar and stir until sugar is dissolved.

7. Transfer pudding to a bowl and let it cool completely.

8. Place in refrigerator until pudding thickens.

9. Serve and enjoy.

Per serving:

Calories 206 Fat 2.9 g Carbohydrates 43.7 g Sugar 27.1g Protein 2.4g Cholesterol 107 mg

Sweetened Breakfast Oats

Prep Time 10 m | Cooking Time 7 m | 4 Servings

Ingredients:

1 cup steel-cut oats

3/4 cup shredded coconut

1/4 tsp ground ginger

1/4 tsp ground nutmeg

1/2 tsp ground cinnamon

1/4 cup raisins

1 large apple, chopped

2 large carrots, grated

1 cup of coconut milk

3 cups of water

Instructions:

1. Add oats, nutmeg, ginger, cinnamon, raisins, apple, carrots, milk, and water

into the instant pot and stir to combine.

2. Seal pot with lid and cook on manual mode for 4 minutes.

3. Once done then allow to release pressure naturally for 20 minutes then

release using the quick-release method. Open the lid.

4. Top with coconut and serve.

Per serving:

Calories 341 Fat 20.8 g Carbohydrates 38.2 g Sugar 16.1 g Protein 5.3 g Cholesterol 0 mg

LUNCH

Low Country Boil

Prep Time 15 m | Cooking Time 10 m | 4 Servings

Ingredients

1/2 pounds (226.8 g) smoked sausages, cut into four pieces

4 ears corn

2 red potatoes cut in half

1 tablespoon (1 tablespoon) Louisiana Shrimp and Crab Boil

Water to cover the above

To add to pot later

1/2 pounds (226.8 g) raw shrimp

For sauce

6 tablespoons (6 tablespoon) Butter

1 tablespoon (1 tablespoon) Garlic, minced

1/8 teaspoon (0.13 teaspoon) Cajun Seasoning

1/4 teaspoons (0.25 teaspoons) Old Bay seasoning

3-5 shakes (3 shakes) Louisiana Hot Sauce, such as Louisiana Hot sauce or Tabasco

1/8 teaspoon (0.13 teaspoons) lemon pepper

1/2 (0.5) Lemon, juiced

Instructions:

1. Place the sausage, corn, and potatoes in the pot and cover with water.

2. Add in the Louisiana Shrimp and Crab Boil Mix.

3. Set your Instant Pot to high pressure for 4 minutes.

4. Meanwhile in a pan over medium-high heat, melt the better.

5. Add minced garlic and sauté well while stirring, allowing the butter to boil and take

on the garlic flavor.

6. Add all other spices and mix well, and taste it. Be sparing with these spices

otherwise, your sauce will get quite salty. Most of the flavor will come from the

butter and garlic, anyway, and you can add the plain hot sauce for heat if you need.

Leave this sauce to warm in the pan. By this time your Instant Pot should be done.

7. Once your Instant Pot is done, perform a Quick Pressure Release, and open the lid

carefully. Check to ensure the potatoes are cooked. Mine were very tender, but not

mushy.

8. Throw in your shrimp and stir. As soon as the shrimp turn pink, take them out, and

then take out the corn, potatoes, and sausage.

9. Put everything a bit into the sauce, stirring well to coat everything with the spiced

butter goodness, starting with the shrimp so they have to cook just a little more.

10. Serve immediately and be prepared for everyone to want to dip their food into the

sauce left in the serving pot.

11. Adjust this as you need to feed children or adults who can't tolerate spice, by simply

relying on butter, garlic, lemon juice, and lemon pepper to add flavor to the butter.

Per serving:

Calories: 459 Carbohydrates: 18g Protein: 22g Fat: 33g

Shrimp and Grits

Prep Time 15 m | Cooking Time 45 m | 4 Servings

Ingredients:

Shrimp Ingredients

1 pound shrimp peeled and deveined

2 teaspoon Old Bay seasoning or more to taste

3 strips smoked bacon diced

1/3 cup onion chopped

1/2 cup bell peppers red and/or green, chopped

1 tablespoon garlic minced

2 tablespoons dry white wine

1 1/2 cups canned diced tomatoes

2 tablespoons lemon juice or to taste

1/4 cup chicken broth

1/4 teaspoon Tabasco sauce or hot sauce, more to taste

1/2 teaspoon salt or to taste

1/4 teaspoon black pepper

1/4 cup heavy cream

1/4 cup scallions sliced thin (green parts only)

Grits Ingredients

1/2 cup grits

1 cup milk

1 cup water

Salt and pepper to taste

1 tablespoon butter optional

Instructions:

1. Pat shrimp dry and sprinkle with Old Bay seasoning. Set aside.

2. On "Sauté" mode, cook bacon until crisp, about 3 minutes. Using a slotted spoon,

remove to a plate and set aside.

3. Sauté onions and bell peppers in the rendered bacon fat till onion is translucent,

about 2 to 3 minutes.

4. Add garlic and sauté briefly. Turn Instant Pot off.

5. Deglaze with white wine, and stir well to remove any browned bits, allowing the

wine to mostly evaporate.

6. Stir in tomatoes, lemon juice, broth, hot sauce, salt and pepper. Place trivet in the

Instant Pot.

7. In a medium bowl that will fit in the Instant Pot, stir together grits, milk, water, salt

and pepper. Place bowl on trivet.

8. Close Instant Pot Lid, and make sure the steam release handle is in the "Sealing"

position.

9. Cook on "Manual" (or "Pressure Cook") mode for 10 minutes. Allow the pressure to

release naturally.

10. Open the Instant Pot, remove the grits and set aside. Remove the trivet. Carefully stir

in shrimp.

11. Close the Instant Pot immediately and allow the shrimp to finish cooking in the

residual heat. Instant Pot will be in "Keep Warm" mode.

12. While shrimp is cooking, fluff grits with a fork, adding in a tablespoon of butter.

13. After 10 minutes, open the Instant Pot. Gently stir the shrimp. Turn on 'Sauté' mode

and stir in cream. Heat through (don't boil) and turn off Instant Pot.

14. Garnish with scallions and bacon. Serve grits topped with shrimp and sauce.

Per serving:

Calories: 292 Carbohydrates: 18g Protein: 30g Fat: 9g

Crust less Crab Quiche

Prep Time 15 m | Cooking Time 50 m | 4 Servings

Ingredients

4 Eggs

1/2 -1 teaspoon Salt

1 teaspoon (1 teaspoon) Ground Black Pepper

1 teaspoon (1 teaspoon) Smoked Paprika

1 teaspoon (1 teaspoon) Herbs de Provence

1 cup (108 g) shredded parmesan or Swiss cheese

1 cup (100 g) Green Onions, green and white parts

8 ounces (226.8 g) imitation crab meat, about 2 cups OR

8 ounces real crab meat, or a mix of crab and chopped raw shrimp

Instructions:

1. In a large bowl, beat together eggs and half-and-half with a whisk. (I don't know if

this will work with non-dairy milk since it needs to set).

2. Add salt, pepper, sweet smoked paprika, Herbs de Provence, and shredded cheese,

and stir with a fork to mix.

3. Stir in chopped green onions.

4. Add in EITHER the imitation crab meat OR the real crab meat OR some

combination of crab meat and chopped raw shrimp. You only want

2 cups of

seafood however you do this

5. Lay out a sheet of aluminum foil that is cut bigger than the pan you intend to use.

Place the spring form pan on this sheet and crimp the sheet about the bottom

6. You are doing this as most spring form pans can leak a little with liquids. The

aluminum foil reduces the mess a little.

7. Pour in the egg mixture into your spring form pan. Cover loosely with foil or a

silicone lid.

8. Into the inner pot of your Instant Pot or pressure cooker, place 2 cups of water. Place

a steamer rack in the pot.

9. Place the covered spring form pan on the trivet. Cook at high pressure for 40

minutes. Let the pot sit undisturbed for 10 minutes and then release all remaining

pressure.

10. Very carefully take out the hot silicone pan. Using a knife, loosen the edges of the

quiche from the pan. Remove the outer ring, and serve your delicious crab quiche

either hot or at room temperature.

Per serving:

Calories: 395 Carbohydrates: 19g Protein: 22g Fat: 25g

Lemon Pepper Salmon

Prep Time 15 m | Cooking Time 10 m | 3-4 Servings

Ingredients:

¾ cup water

A few sprigs of parsley dill, tarragon, basil or a combo

1 pound salmon filet skin on

3 teaspoons ghee or other healthy fat divided

¼ teaspoon salt or to taste

½ teaspoon pepper or to taste

1/2 lemon thinly sliced

1 zucchini julienned

1 red bell pepper julienned

1 carrot julienned

Instructions:

1. Put water and herbs in the Instant Pot and then put in the steamer rack making sure

the handles are extended up.

2. Place salmon, skin down on rack.

3. Drizzle salmon with ghee/fat, season with salt and pepper, and cover with lemon

slices.

4. Close the Instant Pot and make sure the vent is turned to "Sealing". Plug it in, press

"Steam" and press the + or – buttons to set it to 3 minutes.

5. While salmon cooks, julienne your veggies.

6. When the Instant Pot beeps that it's done, quick release the pressure, being careful to

stay out of the way of the steam that will shoot up. Press the "Warm/Cancel" button.

Remove the lid, and using hot pads, carefully remove the rack with salmon and set

on a plate.

7. Remove herbs and discard. Add veggies and put the lid back on. Press "Saute" and

let the veggies cook for just 1 or 2 minutes.

8. Serve veggies with salmon and add remaining teaspoon of fat to the pot and pour a

little of the sauce over them if desired.

Per serving:

Calories: 296 Fat: 15g Carbohydrates 8g Protein: 31g

Shrimp with Tomatoes and Feta

Prep Time 15 m | Cooking Time 12 m | 6 Servings

Ingredients:

Cook Together

2 tablespoons (2 tablespoons) Butter

1 tablespoon (1 tablespoon) Garlic

1/2 teaspoon (0.5 teaspoon) Red Pepper Flakes, adjust to taste

cups (32 g) onions, chopped

1 14.5-oz (1 14.5-oz) Canned Tomatoes

1 teaspoon (1 teaspoon) Dried Oregano

1 teaspoons (1 teaspoons) Salt

1 pound (453.59 g) frozen shrimp, 21-25 count, shelled

Add after cooking

1 cup (150 g) crumbled feta cheese

1/2 cup (67.5 g) sliced black olives

1/4 cup (15 g) Chopped Parsley

Instructions:

1. For the Instant Pot. Turn your Instant Pot or Pressure cooker to "Saute" and once it is

hot, add the butter. Let it melt a little and then add garlic and red pepper flakes.

2. Add in onions, tomatoes, oregano and salt. Pour in the frozen shrimp.

3. Set your Instant pot to "Low" pressure 1 minute. Once the pot is done cooking,

release all pressure immediately.

4. Mix in the shrimp with the rest of the lovely tomato broth. Allow it to cool slightly.

Right before serving, sprinkle the feta cheese, olives, and parsley.

5. This dish makes a soupy broth, so it's great for dipping buttered French bread into, or

eating over rice, or riced cauliflower.

Per serving:

Calories: 211 Carbohydrates: 6g Protein: 19g Fat: 11g

Scallops And Spring Veggies

Prep Time 10 m | Cooking Time 8 m | 4 Servings

Ingredients

½ pound (226.8g) asparagus, ends trimmed, cut into 2-inch pieces

1 cup sugar snap peas

1 pound (453.592g) sea scallops

1 tablespoon lemon juice

2 teaspoons olive oil

½ teaspoon dried thyme

Pinch salt

Freshly ground black pepper

Instructions:

1. Place the asparagus and sugar snap peas in the air fryer basket.

2. Cook for 2 to 3 minutes or until the vegetables are just starting to get tender.

3. Meanwhile, check the scallops for a small muscle attached to the side, and pull it off

and discard.

4. In a medium bowl, toss the scallops with the lemon juice, olive oil, thyme, salt, and

pepper. Place into the air fryer oven basket on top of the

vegetables.

5. Steam for 5 to 7 minutes, tossing the basket once during cooking time, until the

scallops are just firm when tested with your finger and are opaque in the center, and

the vegetables are tender. Serve immediately.

Per serving:

calories: 162; carbs:10g; fat: 4g; protein:22g; fiber:3g

Air Fryer Salmon Patties

Prep Time 8 m | Cooking Time 7 m | 4 Servings

Ingredients

1 tbsp. Olive oil

1 tbsp. Ghee

¼ tsp. Salt

1/8 tsp. Pepper

1 egg

1 c. Almond flour

1 can wild alaskan pink salmon

Instructions:

1. Drain can of salmon into a bowl and keep liquid. Discard skin and bones.

2. Add salt, pepper, and egg to salmon, mixing well with hands to incorporate. Make

patties.

3. Dredge in flour and remaining egg. If it seems dry, spoon reserved salmon liquid

from the can onto patties.

4. Pour the patties into the oven rack/basket. Place the rack on the middle-shelf of the

air fryer oven. Set temperature to 378°f, and set time to 7 minutes. Cook 7 minutes till golden, making sure to flip once during cooking process.

Per serving:

calories: 437; carbs:55; fat: 12g; protein:24g; sugar:2g

Salmon Noodles

Prep Time 5 m | Cooking Time 16 m | 4 Servings

Ingredients

1 salmon fillet

1 tbsp teriyaki marinade

3 ½ ozs soba noodles, cooked and drained

10 ozs firm tofu

7 ozs mixed salad

1 cup broccoli

Olive oil

Salt and pepper to taste

Instructions:

1. Season the salmon with salt and pepper to taste, then coat with the teriyaki marinate.

Set aside for 15 minutes

2. Preheat the air fryer oven at 350 degrees, then cook the salmon for 8 minutes.

3. Whilst the air fryer is cooking the salmon, start slicing the tofu into small cubes.

4. Next, slice the broccoli into smaller chunks. Drizzle with olive oil.

5. Once the salmon is cooked, put the broccoli and tofu into the air fryer oven tray for 8

minutes.

6. Plate the salmon and broccoli tofu mixture over the soba noodles. Add the mixed

salad to the side and serve.

Beer-battered fish and chips

Prep Time 5 m | Cooking Time 30 m | 4 Servings

Ingredients

2 eggs

1 cup malty beer, such as pabst blue ribbon

1 cup all-purpose flour

½ cup cornstarch

1 teaspoon garlic powder

Salt

Pepper

Cooking oil

(4-ounce) cod fillets

Instructions:

1 In a medium bowl, beat the eggs with the beer. In another medium bowl, combine the

flour and cornstarch, and season with the garlic powder and salt and pepper to taste.

2 Spray the air fryer basket with cooking oil.

3 Dip each cod fillet in the flour and cornstarch mixture and then in the egg and beer

mixture. Dip the cod in the flour and cornstarch a second time.

4 Place the cod in the air fryer oven. Do not stack. Cook in batches. Spray with cooking oil.

Cook for 8 minutes.

5 Open the air fryer oven and flip the cod. Cook for an additional 7 minutes.

6 Remove the cooked cod from the air fryer, then repeat steps 4 and 5 for the remaining

fillets.

7 Serve with prepared air fried frozen fries. Frozen fries will need to be cooked for 18 to 20

minutes at 400°f.

8 Cool before serving.

Per serving:

calories: 325; carbs:41; fat: 4g; protein:26g; fiber:1g

Tuna Stuffed Potatoes

Prep Time 5 m | Cooking Time 30 m | 4 Servings

Ingredients

4 starchy potatoes

½ tablespoon olive oil

1 (6-ounce) can tuna, drained

2 tablespoons plain greek yogurt

1 teaspoon red chili powder

Salt and freshly ground black pepper, to taste

1 scallion, chopped and divided

1 tablespoon capers

Instructions:

In a large bowl of water, soak the potatoes for about 30 minutes. Drain well and pat

dry with paper towel.

Preheat the air fryer to 355 degrees f. Place the potatoes in a fryer basket.

Cook for about 30 minutes.

Meanwhile in a bowl, add tuna, yogurt, red chili powder, salt, black pepper and half

of scallion and with a potato masher, mash the mixture completely.

Remove the potatoes from the air fryer oven and place onto a smooth surface.

Carefully, cut each potato from top side lengthwise.

With your fingers, press the open side of potato halves slightly. Stuff the potato open

portion with tuna mixture evenly.

Sprinkle with the capers and remaining scallion. Serve immediately.

Per serving:

Calories: 795, Protein: 109.77g, Fat: g, Carbs: g

Fried Calamari

Prep Time 8 m | Cooking Time 7 m | 6-8 Servings

Ingredients

½ tsp. Salt

½ tsp. Old bay seasoning

1/3 c. Plain cornmeal

½ c. Semolina flour

½ c. Almond flour

5-6 c. Olive oil

1 ½ pounds (680.389g) baby squid

Instructions:

1 Rinse squid in cold water and slice tentacles, keeping just ¼-inch of the hood in one

piece.

2 Combine 1-2 pinches of pepper, salt, old bay seasoning, cornmeal, and both flours

together. Dredge squid pieces into flour mixture and place into the air fryer basket.

3 Spray liberally with olive oil. Cook 15 minutes at 345 degrees till coating turns a golden

brown.

Per serving:

Calories: 211; carbs:55; fat: 6g; protein:21g; sugar:1g

Soy And Ginger Shrimp

Prep Time 8 m | Cooking Time 10 m | 4 Servings

Ingredients

2 tablespoons olive oil

2 tablespoons scallions, finely chopped

2 cloves garlic, chopped

1 teaspoon fresh ginger, grated

1 tablespoon dry white wine

1 tablespoon balsamic vinegar

1/4 cup soy sauce

1 tablespoon sugar

1 pound (453.592g) shrimp

Salt and ground black pepper, to taste

Instructions:

To make the marinade, warm the oil in a saucepan; cook all ingredients, except the

shrimp, salt, and black pepper. Now, let it cool.

Marinate the shrimp, covered, at least an hour, in the refrigerator.

After that, pour into the oven rack/basket. Place the rack on the middle-shelf of the

air fryer oven. Set temperature to 350°f, and set time to 10 minutes. Bake the shrimp

at 350 degrees f for 8 to 10 minutes (depending on the size), turning once or twice.

Season prepared shrimp with salt and black pepper and serve.

Per serving:

Calories: 233, Protein: 24.55g, Fat: 10.28g, Carbs: 10.86g

Crispy Cheesy Fish Fingers

Prep Time 10 m | Cooking Time 20 m | 4 Servings

Ingredients

Large cod fish filet, approximately 6-8 ounces, fresh or frozen and thawed, cut into 1

½-inch strips

2 raw eggs

½ cup of breadcrumbs (we like panko, but any brand or home recipe will do)

2 tablespoons of shredded or powdered parmesan cheese

1 tablespoons of shredded cheddar cheese

Pinch of salt and pepper

Instructions:

1 Cover the basket of the air fryer oven with a lining of tin foil, leaving the edges

uncovered to allow air to circulate through the basket.

2 Preheat the air fryer oven to 350 degrees.

3 In a large mixing bowl, beat the eggs until fluffy and until the yolks and whites are fully

combined.

4 Dunk all the fish strips in the beaten eggs, fully submerging.

5 In a separate mixing bowl, combine the bread crumbs with the parmesan, cheddar, and

salt and pepper, until evenly mixed.

6 One by one, coat the egg-covered fish strips in the mixed dry ingredients so that they're

fully covered, and place on the foil-lined air fryer basket.

7 Set the air fryer oven timer to 20 minutes.

8 Halfway through the cooking time, shake the handle of the air fryer so that the breaded

fish jostles inside and fry coverage is even.

9 After 20 minutes, when the fryer shuts off, the fish strips will be perfectly cooked and

their breaded crust golden-brown and delicious! Using tongs, remove from the air fryer

and set on a serving dish to cool.

Per serving:

Calories: 124, Protein: 6.86g, Fat: 5.93g, Carbs: 12.26g

Panko-Crusted Tilapia

Prep Time 5 m | Cooking Time 10 m | 3 Servings

Ingredients

2 tsp. Italian seasoning

2 tsp. Lemon pepper

1/3 c. Panko breadcrumbs

1/3 c. Egg whites

1/3 c. Almond flour

tilapia fillets

Olive oil

Instructions:

1 Place panko, egg whites, and flour into separate bowls. Mix lemon pepper and italian

seasoning in with breadcrumbs.

2 Pat tilapia fillets dry. Dredge in flour, then egg, then breadcrumb mixture.

3 Add to the air fryer basket and spray lightly with olive oil.

4 Cook 10-11 minutes at 400 degrees, making sure to flip halfway through cooking.

Per serving:

Calories: 256; fat: 9g; protein:39g; sugar:5g

Potato Crusted Salmon

Prep Time 10 m | Cooking Time 15 m | 4 Servings

Ingredients

1 pound (453.592g) salmon, swordfish or arctic char fillets, 3/4 inch thick

1 egg white

2 tablespoons water

1/3 cup dry instant mashed potatoes

2 teaspoons cornstarch

1 teaspoon paprika

1 teaspoon lemon pepper seasoning

Instructions:

1 Remove and skin from the fish and cut it into 4 serving pieces mix together the egg white

and water. Mix together all of the dry ingredients. Dip the filets into the egg white

mixture then press into the potato mix to coat evenly.

2 Pour into the oven rack/basket. Place the rack on the middle-shelf of the air fryer oven.

Set temperature to 360°f, and set time to 15 minutes, flip the filets halfway through.

Per serving:

Calories:176; fat: 7g; protein:23g; :5g

Salmon Croquettes

Prep Time 5 m | Cooking Time 10 m | 6-8 Servings

Ingredients

Panko breadcrumbs

Almond flour

egg whites

2 tbsp. Chopped chives

2 tbsp. Minced garlic cloves

½ c. Chopped onion

2/3 c. Grated carrots

1 pound (453.592g) chopped salmon fillet

Instructions:

1 Mix together all ingredients minus breadcrumbs, flour, and egg whites.

2 Shape mixture into balls. Then coat them in flour, then egg, and then breadcrumbs.

Drizzle with olive oil.

3 Pour the coated salmon balls into the oven rack/basket. Place the rack on the middle-shelf

of the air fryer oven. Set temperature to 350°f, and set time to 6 minutes. Shake and

cook an additional 4 minutes until golden in color.

Per serving:

Calories: 503 carbs:61g fat: 9g; protein:5g; sugar:4g

Snapper Scampi

Prep Time 5 m | Cooking Time 10 m | 4 Servings

Ingredients

(6-ounce) skinless snapper or arctic char fillets

1 tablespoon olive oil

tablespoons lemon juice, divided

½ teaspoon dried basil

Pinch salt

Freshly ground black pepper

2 tablespoons butter

Cloves garlic, minced

Instructions:

1 Rub the fish fillets with olive oil and 1 tablespoon of the lemon juice. Sprinkle with the

basil, salt, and pepper, and place in the air fryer oven basket.

2 Grill the fish for 7 to 8 minutes or until the fish just flakes when tested with a fork.

Remove the fish from the basket and put on a serving plate. Cover to keep warm. In a 6-

by-6-by-2-inch pan, combine the butter, remaining 2 tablespoons lemon juice, and

garlic. Cook in the air fryer oven for 1 to 2 minutes or until the garlic is sizzling. Pour this mixture over the fish and serve.

Per serving:

Calories: 265; carbs:1g; fat: 11g; protein:39g; fiber:0g

Thai Fish Cakes With Mango Relish

Prep Time 5 m | Cooking Time 10 m | 4 Servings

Ingredients

1 lb (453.592g) white fish fillets

tbsps ground coconut

1 ripened mango

½ tsps chili paste

Tbsps fresh parsley

1 green onion

1 lime

1 tsp salt

1 egg

Instructions:

1 To make the relish, peel and dice the mango into cubes. Combine with a half teaspoon of

chili paste, a tablespoon of parsley, and the zest and juice of half a lime.

2 In a food processor, pulse the fish until it forms a smooth texture. Place into a bowl and

add the salt, egg, chopped green onion, parsley, two tablespoons of the coconut, and the

remainder of the chili paste and lime zest and juice. Combine well

3 Portion the mixture into 10 equal balls and flatten them into small patties. Pour the

reserved tablespoon of coconut onto a dish and roll the patties over to coat.

4 Preheat the air fryer oven to 390 degrees

5 Place the fish cakes into the air fryer oven and cook for 8 minutes. They should be crisp

and lightly browned when ready

6 Serve hot with mango relish

Per serving:

Air Fryer Fish Tacos

Prep Time 5 m | Cooking Time 15 m | 4 Servings

Ingredients

1 pound (453.592g) cod

1 tbsp. Cumin

½ tbsp. Chili powder

1 ½ c. Almond flour

1 ½ c. Coconut flour

ounces mexican beer

eggs

Instructions:

1 Whisk beer and eggs together.

2 Whisk flours, pepper, salt, cumin, and chili powder together.

3 Slice cod into large pieces and coat in egg mixture then flour mixture.

4 Spray bottom of your air fryer oven basket with olive oil and add coated codpieces. Cook

15 minutes at 375 degrees.

5 Serve on lettuce leaves topped with homemade salsa.

Per serving:

Calories: 178; carbs:61g; fat:10g; protein:19g; sugar:1g

Firecracker shrimp

Prep Time 10 m | Cooking Time 8 m | 4 Servings

Ingredients

For the shrimp

1 pound (453.592g) raw shrimp, peeled and deveined

Salt

Pepper

1 egg

½ cup all-purpose flour

¾ cup panko bread crumbs

Cooking oil

For the firecracker sauce

⅓ cup sour cream

tablespoons sriracha

¼ cup sweet chili sauce

Instructions:

1 Season the shrimp with salt and pepper to taste. In a small bowl, beat the egg. In another

small bowl, place the flour. In a third small bowl, add the panko bread crumbs.

2 Spray the air fryer oven basket with cooking oil. Dip the shrimp in the flour, then the egg,

and then the bread crumbs. Place the shrimp in the air fryer basket. It is okay to stack them. Spray the shrimp with cooking oil.

3 Cook for 4 minutes. Open the air fryer oven and flip the shrimp. I recommend flipping individually instead of shaking to keep the breading intact. Cook for an additional 4 minutes or until crisp.

4 While the shrimp is cooking, make the firecracker sauce: in a small bowl, combine the sour cream, sriracha, and sweet chili sauce. Mix well. Serve with the shrimp.

Per serving:

Calories: 266; carbs:23g; fat:6g; protein:27g; fiber:1g

Sesame Seeds Coated Fish

Prep Time 10 m | Cooking Time 8 m | 5 Servings

Ingredients

tablespoons plain flour

eggs

½ cup sesame seeds, toasted

½ cup breadcrumbs

1/8 teaspoon dried rosemary, crushed

Pinch of salt

Pinch of black pepper

tablespoons olive oil

frozen fish fillets (white fish of your choice)

Instructions:

1 In a shallow dish, place flour. In a second shallow dish, beat the eggs. In a third shallow

dish, add remaining ingredients except fish fillets and mix till a crumbly mixture forms.

2 Coat the fillets with flour and shake off the excess flour.

3 Next, dip the fillets in egg.

4 Then coat the fillets with sesame seeds mixture generously.

5 Preheat the air fryer oven to 390 degrees f.

6 Line an air fryer basket with a piece of foil. Arrange the fillets into prepared basket.

7 Cook for about 14 minutes, flipping once after 10 minutes.

Per serving:

Calories: 393, Protein: 13.41g, Fat: 30.44g, Carbs: 18.09g

DINNER

Turkey Breasts with Greek Mustard Sauce

Prep Time 1 h 13 m | Cooking Time 18 m | 4 Servings

Ingredients:

1/2 teaspoon cumin powder

2 pounds turkey breasts, quartered

2 cloves garlic, smashed

½ teaspoon hot paprika

2 tablespoons melted butter

1 teaspoon fine sea salt

Freshly cracked mixed peppercorns, to savor

Fresh juice of 1 lemon

For the mustard sauce:

1 ½ tablespoons mayonnaise

1 ½ cups Greek yogurt

1/2 tablespoon yellow mustard

Instructions:

1. Grab a medium-sized mixing dish and combine the garlic and melted butter; rub this

mixture evenly over the surface of the turkey.

2. Add the cumin powder, followed by paprika, salt, peppercorns, and lemon juice.

Place in your refrigerator at least 55 minutes.

3. Set your air fryer to cook at 375 degrees f. Roast the turkey for 18 minutes, turning

halfway through; roast in batches.

4. In the meantime, make the mustard sauce by mixing all ingredients for the sauce.

Serve warm roasted turkey with the mustard sauce.

Per serving:

Calories 471 Fat 20.3 g Carbohydrates 1.5 g Sugar 0 g Protein 45.2 g Cholesterol 139 mg

Country-Style Nutty Turkey Breast

Prep Time 30 m | Cooking Time 25 m | 2 Servings

Ingredients:

1 ½ tablespoons coconut amines

1/2 tablespoon xanthan gum

2 bay leaves

1/3 cup dry sherry

1 ½ tablespoons chopped walnuts

1 teaspoon shallot powder

1-pound turkey breasts, sliced

1 teaspoon garlic powder

2 teaspoons olive oil

1/2 teaspoon onion salt

1/2 teaspoon red pepper flakes, crushed

1 teaspoon ground black pepper

Instructions:

1. Begin by preheating your air fryer to 395 degrees f. Place all ingredients, minus

chopped walnuts, in a mixing bowl and let them marinate at least 1 hour.

2. After that, cook the marinated turkey breast approximately 23

minutes or until heated

through.

3. Pause the machine, scatter chopped walnuts over the top and air-fry an additional 5

minutes.

Per serving:

Calories 365 Fat 20.3 g Carbohydrates 1.5 g Sugar 0 g Protein 45.2 g Cholesterol 139 mg

Eggs and Sausage with Keto Rolls

Prep Time 40 m | Cooking Time 14 m | 6 Servings

Ingredients:

1 teaspoon dried dill weed

1 teaspoon mustard seeds

6 turkey sausages

3 bell peppers, seeded and thinly sliced

6 medium-sized eggs

1/2 teaspoon fennel seeds

1 teaspoon sea salt

1/3 teaspoon freshly cracked pink peppercorns

Keto rolls:

1/2 cup ricotta cheese, crumbled

1 cup part skim mozzarella cheese, shredded

1 egg

1/2 cup coconut flour

1/2 cup almond flour

1 teaspoon baking soda

2 tablespoons plain whey protein isolate

Instructions:

1. Set your air fryer to cook at 325 degrees f. Cook the sausages and bell peppers in the

air fryer cooking basket for 8 minutes.

2. Crack the eggs into the ramekins; sprinkle them with salt, dill weed, mustard seeds,

fennel seeds, and cracked peppercorns. Cook an additional 12 minutes at 395 degrees

f.

3. To make the keto rolls, microwave the cheese for 1 minute 30 seconds, stirring twice.

Add the cheese to the bowl of a food processor and blend well. Fold in the egg and

mix again.

4. Add in the flour, baking soda, and plain whey protein isolate; blend again. Scrape the

batter onto the center of a lightly greased cling film.

5. Form the dough into a disk and transfer to your freezer to cool; cut into 6 pieces and

transfer to a parchment-lined baking pan (make sure to grease your hands.

6. Bake in the preheated oven at 400 degrees f for about 14 minutes.

7. Serve eggs and sausages on keto rolls.

Per serving:

Calories 398 Fat 20.3 g Carbohydrates 1.5 g Sugar 0 g Protein 45.2 g Cholesterol 139 mg

Bacon-Wrapped Turkey with Cheese

Prep Time 20 m | Cooking Time 13 m | 12 Servings

Ingredients:

1 ½ small-sized turkey breast, chop into 12 pieces

12 thin slices asiago cheese

Paprika, to taste

Fine sea salt and ground black pepper, to savor

12 rashers bacon

Instructions:

1. Lay out the bacon rashers; place 1 slice of asiago cheese on each bacon piece.

2. Top with turkey, season with paprika, salt, and pepper, and roll them up; secure with

a cocktail stick.

3. Air-fry at 365 degrees f for 13 minutes.

Per serving:

Calories 534 Fat 20.3 g Carbohydrates 1.5 g Sugar 0 g Protein 45.2 g Cholesterol 139 mg

Italian-Style Spicy Chicken Breasts

Prep Time 20 m | Cooking Time 11 m | 4 Servings

Ingredients:

2 ounces asiago cheese, cut into sticks

1/3 cup tomato paste

1/2 teaspoon garlic paste

2 chicken breasts, cut in half lengthwise

1/2 cup green onions, chopped

1 tablespoon chili sauce

1/2 cup roasted vegetable stock

1 tablespoon sesame oil

1 teaspoon salt

2 teaspoons unsweetened cocoa

1/2 teaspoon sweet paprika, or more to taste

Instructions:

1. Sprinkle chicken breasts with the salt and sweet paprika; drizzle with chili sauce.

Now, place a stick of asiago cheese in the middle of each chicken breast.

2. Then, tie the whole thing using a kitchen string; give a drizzle of sesame oil.

3. Transfer the stuffed chicken to the cooking basket. Add the other ingredients and toss

to coat the chicken.

4. Afterward, cook for about 11 minutes at 395 degrees f. Serve the chicken on two

serving plates, garnish with fresh or pickled salad and serve immediately.

Per serving:

Calories 398 Fat 20.3 g Carbohydrates 1.5 g Sugar 0 g Protein 45.2 g Cholesterol 139 mg

Classic Chicken Nuggets

Prep Time 20 m | Cooking Time 10 m | 4 Servings

Ingredients:

1 ½ pounds chicken tenderloins, cut into small pieces

1/2 teaspoon garlic salt

1/2 teaspoon cayenne pepper

1/4 teaspoon black pepper, freshly cracked

4 tablespoons olive oil

2 scoops low-carb unflavored protein powder

4 tablespoons parmesan cheese, freshly grated

Instructions:

1. Start by preheating your air fryer to 390 degrees f.

2. Season each piece of the chicken with garlic salt, cayenne pepper, and black pepper.

3. In a mixing bowl, thoroughly combine the olive oil with protein powder and

parmesan cheese. Dip each piece of chicken in the parmesan mixture.

4. Cook for 8 minutes, working in batches.

5. Later, if you want to warm the chicken nuggets, add them to the basket and cook for

1 minute more.

Per serving:

Calories 327 Fat 20.3 g Carbohydrates 1.5 g Sugar 0 g Protein 45.2 g Cholesterol 139 mg

Thai Chicken with Bacon

Prep Time 50 m | Cooking Time 20 m | 2 Servings

Ingredients:

4 rashers smoked bacon

2 chicken filets

1/2 teaspoon coarse sea salt

1/4 teaspoon black pepper, preferably freshly ground

1 teaspoon garlic, minced

1 (2-inch piece ginger, peeled and minced

1 teaspoon black mustard seeds

1 teaspoon mild curry powder

1/2 cup coconut milk

1/2 cup parmesan cheese, grated

Instructions:

1. Start by preheating your air fryer to 400 degrees f. Add the smoked bacon and cook

in the preheated air fryer for 5 to 7 minutes. Reserve.

2. In a mixing bowl, place the chicken fillets, salt, black pepper, garlic, ginger, mustard

seeds, curry powder, and milk. Let it marinate in your refrigerator about 30 minutes.

3. In another bowl, place the grated parmesan cheese.

4. Dredge the chicken fillets through the parmesan mixture and

transfer them to the

cooking basket. Reduce the temperature to 380 degrees f and cook the chicken for 6

minutes.

5. Turn them over and cook for a further 6 minutes. Repeat the process until you have

run out of ingredients.

6. Serve with reserved bacon. Enjoy!

Per serving:

Calories 612 Fat 20.3 g Carbohydrates 1.5 g Sugar 0 g Protein 45.2 g Cholesterol 139 mg

Thanksgiving Turkey with Mustard Gravy

Prep Time 50 m | Cooking Time 45 m | 6 Servings

Ingredients:

2 teaspoons butter, softened

1 teaspoon dried sage

2 sprigs rosemary, chopped

1 teaspoon salt

1/4 teaspoon freshly ground black pepper, or more to taste

1 whole turkey breast

2 tablespoons turkey broth

2 tablespoons whole-grain mustard

1 tablespoon butter

Instructions:

1. Start by preheating your air fryer to 360 degrees f.

2. To make the rub, combine 2 tablespoons of butter, sage, rosemary, salt, and pepper;

mix well to combine and spread it evenly over the surface of the turkey breast.

3. Roast for 20 minutes in an air fryer cooking basket. Flip the turkey breast over and

cook for a further 15 to 16 minutes. Now, flip it back over and roast for 12 minutes more.

4. While the turkey is roasting, whisk the other ingredients in a saucepan. After that,

spread the gravy all over the turkey breast.

5. Let the turkey rest for a few minutes before carving.

Per serving:

Calories 376 Fat 20.3 g Carbohydrates 1.5 g Sugar 0 g Protein 45.2 g Cholesterol 139 mg

Pretzel Crusted Chicken With Spicy Mustard Sauce

Prep Time 15 m | Cooking Time 20 m | 6 Servings

Ingredients:

2 eggs

1 ½ pound chicken breasts, boneless, skinless, cut into bite-sized chunks

1/2 cup crushed pretzels

1 teaspoon shallot powder

1 teaspoon paprika

Sea salt and ground black pepper, to taste

1/2 cup vegetable broth

1 tablespoon cornstarch

3 tablespoons Worcestershire sauce

3 tablespoons tomato paste

1 tablespoon apple cider vinegar

2 tablespoons olive oil

2 garlic cloves, chopped

1 jalapeno pepper, minced

1 teaspoon yellow mustard

Instructions:

1. Start by preheating your Air Fryer to 390 degrees F.

2. In a mixing dish, whisk the eggs until frothy; toss the chicken chunks into the

whisked eggs and coat well.

3. In another dish, combine the crushed pretzels with shallot powder, paprika, salt and

pepper. Then, lay the chicken chunks in the pretzel mixture; turn it over until well

coated.

4. Place the chicken pieces in the air fryer basket. Cook the chicken for 12 minutes,

shaking the basket halfway through.

5. Meanwhile, whisk the vegetable broth with cornstarch, Worcestershire sauce, tomato

paste, and apple cider vinegar.

6. Preheat a cast-iron skillet over medium flame. Heat the olive oil and sauté the garlic

with jalapeno pepper for 30 to 40 seconds, stirring frequently.

7. Add the cornstarch mixture and let it simmer until the sauce has thickened a little.

Now, add the air-fried chicken and mustard; let it simmer for 2 minutes more or until

heated through.

8. Serve immediately and enjoy!

Per serving:

357 Calories 17.6g Fat 20.3g Carbs 28.1g Protein 2.8g Sugars

Chinese-Style Sticky Turkey Thighs

Prep Time 20 m | Cooking Time 35 m | 6 Servings

Ingredients:

1 tablespoon sesame oil

2 pounds turkey thighs

1 teaspoon Chinese Five-spice powder

1 teaspoon pink Himalayan salt

1/4 teaspoon Sichuan pepper

6 tablespoons honey

1 tablespoon Chinese rice vinegar

2 tablespoons soy sauce

1 tablespoon sweet chili sauce

1 tablespoon mustard

Instructions:

1. Preheat your Air Fryer to 360 degrees F.

2. Brush the sesame oil all over the turkey thighs. Season them with spices.

3. Cook for 23 minutes, turning over once or twice. Make sure to work in batches to

ensure even cooking

4. In the meantime, combine the remaining ingredients in a wok

(or similar type pan)

that is preheated over medium-high heat. Cook and stir until the sauce reduces by

about a third.

5. Add the fried turkey thighs to the wok; gently stir to coat with the sauce.

6. Let the turkey rest for 10 minutes before slicing and serving. Enjoy!

Per serving:

279 Calories 10.1g Fat 19g Carbs 27.7g Protein 17.9g Sugars

Easy Hot Chicken Drumsticks

Prep Time 40 m | Cooking Time 30 m | 6 Servings

Ingredients:

6 chicken drumsticks

Sauce:

6 ounces hot sauce

3 tablespoons olive oil

3 tablespoons tamari sauce

1 teaspoon dried thyme

1/2 teaspoon dried oregano

Instructions:

1. Spritz the sides and bottom of the cooking basket with a nonstick cooking spray.

2. Cook the chicken drumsticks at 380 degrees F for 35 minutes, flipping them over

halfway through.

3. Meanwhile, heat the hot sauce, olive oil, tamari sauce, thyme, and oregano in a pan

over medium-low heat; reserve.

4. Drizzle the sauce over the prepared chicken drumsticks; toss to coat well and serve.

Bon appétit!

Per serving:

280 Calories 18.7g Fat 2.6g Carbs 24.1g Protein 1.4g Sugars

Crunchy Munchy Chicken Tenders With Peanuts

Prep Time 25 m | Cooking Time 20 m | 4 Servings

Ingredients:

1 ½ pounds chicken tenderloins

2 tablespoons peanut oil

1/2 cup tortilla chips, crushed

Sea salt and ground black pepper, to taste

1/2 teaspoon garlic powder

1 teaspoon red pepper flakes

2 tablespoons peanuts, roasted and roughly chopped

Instructions:

1. Start by preheating your Air Fryer to 360 degrees F.

2. Brush the chicken tenderloins with peanut oil on all sides.

3. In a mixing bowl, thoroughly combine the crushed chips, salt, black pepper, garlic

powder, and red pepper flakes. Dredge the chicken in the breading, shaking off any

residual coating.

4. Lay the chicken tenderloins into the cooking basket. Cook for 12 to 13 minutes or

until it is no longer pink in the center. Work in batches; an instant-read thermometer should read at least 165 degrees F.

5. Serve garnished with roasted peanuts. Bon appétit!

Per serving:

343 Calories 16.4g Fat 10.6g Carbs 36.8g Protein 1g Sugar

Tarragon Turkey Tenderloins With Baby Potatoes

Prep Time 50 m | Cooking Time 50 m | 6 Servings

Ingredients:

2 pounds turkey tenderloins

2 teaspoons olive oil

Salt and ground black pepper, to taste

1 teaspoon smoked paprika

2 tablespoons dry white wine

1 tablespoon fresh tarragon leaves, chopped

1-pound baby potatoes, rubbed

Instructions:

1. Brush the turkey tenderloins with olive oil. Season with salt, black pepper, and

paprika.

2. Afterwards, add the white wine and tarragon.

3. Cook the turkey tenderloins at 350 degrees F for 30 minutes, flipping them over

halfway through. Let them rest for 5 to 9 minutes before slicing and serving.

4. After that, spritz the sides and bottom of the cooking basket with the remaining 1

teaspoon of olive oil.

5. Then, preheat your Air Fryer to 400 degrees F; cook the baby potatoes for 15

minutes. Serve with the turkey and enjoy!

Per serving:

317 Calories 7.4g Fat 14.2g Carbs 45.7g Protein 1.1g Sugars

Mediterranean Chicken Breasts With Roasted Tomatoes

Prep Time 1 h | Cooking Time 30 m | 8 Servings

Ingredients:

2 teaspoons olive oil, melted

3 pounds chicken breasts, bone-in

1/2 teaspoon black pepper, freshly ground

1/2 teaspoon salt

1 teaspoon cayenne pepper

2 tablespoons fresh parsley, minced

1 teaspoon fresh basil, minced

1 teaspoon fresh rosemary, minced

4 medium-sized Roma tomatoes, halved

Instructions:

1. Start by preheating your Air Fryer to 370 degrees F. Brush the cooking basket with 1

teaspoon of olive oil.

2. Sprinkle the chicken breasts with all seasonings listed above.

3. Cook for 25 minutes or until chicken breasts are slightly browned. Work in batches.

4. Arrange the tomatoes in the cooking basket and brush them

with the remaining

teaspoon of olive oil. Season with sea salt.

5. Cook the tomatoes at 350 degrees F for 10 minutes, shaking halfway through the

cooking time. Serve with chicken breasts. Bon appétit!

Per serving:

315 Calories 17.1g Fat 2.7g Carbs 36g Protein 1.7g Sugars

Thai Red Duck With Candy Onion

Prep Time 25 m | Cooking Time 25 m | 4 Servings

Ingredients:

1 ½ pounds duck breasts, skin removed

1 teaspoon kosher salt

1/2 teaspoon cayenne pepper

1/3 teaspoon black pepper

1/2 teaspoon smoked paprika

1 tablespoon Thai red curry paste

1 cup candy onions, halved

1/4 small pack coriander, chopped

Instructions:

1. Place the duck breasts between 2 sheets of foil; then, use a rolling pin to bash the

duck until they are 1-inch thick.

2. Preheat your Air Fryer to 395 degrees F.

3. Rub the duck breasts with salt, cayenne pepper, black pepper, paprika, and red curry

paste. Place the duck breast in the cooking basket.

4. Cook for 11 to 12 minutes. Top with candy onions and cook for another 10 to 11

minutes.

5. Serve garnished with coriander and enjoy!

Per serving:

362 Calories 18.7g Fat 4g Carbs 42.3g Protein 1.3g Sugars

Rustic Chicken Legs With Turnip Chips

Prep Time 30 m | Cooking Time 20 m | 3 Servings

Ingredients:

1-pound chicken legs

1 teaspoon Himalayan salt

1 teaspoon paprika

1/2 teaspoon ground black pepper

1 teaspoon butter, melted

1 turnip, trimmed and sliced

Instructions:

1. Spritz the sides and bottom of the cooking basket with a nonstick cooking spray.

2. Season the chicken legs with salt, paprika, and ground black pepper.

3. Cook at 370 degrees F for 10 minutes. Increase the temperature to 380 degrees F.

4. Drizzle turnip slices with melted butter and transfer them to the cooking basket with

the chicken. Cook the turnips and chicken for 15 minutes more, flipping them

halfway through the cooking time.

5. As for the chicken, an instant-read thermometer should read at least 165 degrees F.

6. Serve and enjoy!

Per serving:

207 Calories 7.8g Fat 3.4g Carbs 29.5g Protein 1.6g Sugars

Old-Fashioned Chicken Drumettes

Prep Time 30 m | Cooking Time 22 m | 3 Servings

Ingredients:

1/3 cup all-purpose flour

1/2 teaspoon ground white pepper

1 teaspoon seasoning salt

1 teaspoon garlic paste

1 teaspoon rosemary

1 whole egg + 1 egg white

6 chicken drumettes

1 heaping tablespoon fresh chives, chopped

Instructions:

1. Start by preheating your Air Fryer to 390 degrees.

2. Mix the flour with white pepper, salt, garlic paste, and rosemary in a small-sized

bowl.

3. In another bowl, beat the eggs until frothy.

4. Dip the chicken into the flour mixture, then into the beaten eggs; coat with the flour

mixture one more time.

5. Cook the chicken drumettes for 22 minutes. Serve warm,

garnished with chives.

Per serving:

347 Calories 9.1g Fat 11.3g Carbs 41g Protein 0.1g Sugars

Easy Ritzy Chicken Nuggets

Prep Time 20 m | Cooking Time 8 m | 4 Servings

Ingredients:

1 ½ pounds chicken tenderloins, cut into small pieces

1/2 teaspoon garlic salt

1/2 teaspoon cayenne pepper

1/4 teaspoon black pepper, freshly cracked

4 tablespoons olive oil

1/3 cup saltines (e.g. Ritz crackers), crushed

4 tablespoons Parmesan cheese, freshly grated

Instructions:

1. Start by preheating your Air Fryer to 390 degrees F.

2. Season each piece of the chicken with garlic salt, cayenne pepper, and black pepper.

3. In a mixing bowl, thoroughly combine the olive oil with crushed saltines. Dip each

piece of chicken in the cracker mixture.

4. Finally, roll the chicken pieces over the Parmesan cheese. Cook for 8 minutes,

working in batches.

5. Later, if you want to warm the chicken nuggets, add them to the basket and cook for

1 minute more. Serve with French fries, if desired.

Per serving:

355 Calories 20.1g Fat 5.3g Carbs 36.6g Protein 0.2g Sugars

Asian Chicken Filets With Cheese

Prep Time 50 m | Cooking Time 20 m | 2 Servings

Ingredients:

4 rashers smoked bacon

2 chicken filets

1/2 teaspoon coarse sea salt

1/4 teaspoon black pepper, preferably freshly ground

1 teaspoon garlic, minced

1 (2-inch) piece ginger, peeled and minced

1 teaspoon black mustard seeds

1 teaspoon mild curry powder

1/2 cup coconut milk

1/3 cup tortilla chips, crushed

1/2 cup Pecorino Romano cheese, freshly grated

Instructions:

1. Start by preheating your Air Fryer to 400 degrees F. Add the smoked bacon and cook

in the preheated Air Fryer for 5 to 7 minutes. Reserve.

2. In a mixing bowl, place the chicken fillets, salt, black pepper, garlic, ginger, mustard

seeds, curry powder, and milk. Let it marinate in your refrigerator about 30 minutes.

3. In another bowl, mix the crushed chips and grated Pecorino Romano cheese.

4. Dredge the chicken fillets through the chips mixture and transfer them to the cooking

basket. Reduce the temperature to 380 degrees F and cook the chicken for 6 minutes.

5. Turn them over and cook for a further 6 minutes. Repeat the process until you have

run out of ingredients.

6. Serve with reserved bacon. Enjoy!

Per serving:

376 Calories 19.6g Fat 12.1g Carbs 36.2g Protein 3.4g Sugars

72

Paprika Chicken Legs With Brussels Sprouts

Prep Time 30 m | Cooking Time 20 m | 2 Servings

Ingredients:

2 chicken legs

1/2 teaspoon paprika

1/2 teaspoon kosher salt

1/2 teaspoon black pepper

1-pound Brussels sprouts

1 teaspoon dill, fresh or dried

Instructions:

1. Start by preheating your Air Fryer to 370 degrees F.

2. Now, season your chicken with paprika, salt, and pepper. Transfer the chicken legs to

the cooking basket. Cook for 10 minutes.

3. Flip the chicken legs and cook an additional 10 minutes. Reserve.

4. Add the Brussels sprouts to the cooking basket; sprinkle with dill. Cook at 380

degrees F for 15 minutes, shaking the basket halfway through.

5. Serve with the reserved chicken legs. Bon appétit!

Per serving:

Chinese Duck

Prep Time 30 m | Cooking Time 20 m | 6 Servings

Ingredients:

2 pounds duck breast, boneless

2 green onions, chopped

1 tablespoon light soy sauce

1 teaspoon Chinese 5-spice powder

1 teaspoon Szechuan peppercorns

3 tablespoons Shaoxing rice wine

1 teaspoon coarse salt

1/2 teaspoon ground black pepper

Glaze:

1/4 cup molasses

3 tablespoons orange juice

1 tablespoon soy sauce

Instructions:

1. In a ceramic bowl, place the duck breasts, green onions, light soy sauce, Chinese 5-

spice powder, Szechuan peppercorns, and Shaoxing rice wine. Let it marinate for 1

hour in your refrigerator.

2. Preheat your Air Fryer to 400 degrees F for 5 minutes.

3. Now, discard the marinade and season the duck breasts with salt and pepper. Cook

the duck breasts for 12 to 15 minutes or until they are golden brown. Repeat with the

other ingredients.

4. In the meantime, add the reserved marinade to the saucepan that is preheated over

medium-high heat. Add the molasses, orange juice, and 1 tablespoon of soy sauce.

5. Bring to a simmer and then, whisk constantly until it gets syrupy. Brush the surface

of duck breasts with glaze so they are completely covered.

6. Place duck breasts back in the Air Fryer basket; cook an additional 5 minutes. Enjoy!

Per serving:

403 Calories 25.3g Fat 16.4g Carbs 27.5g Protein 13.2g Sugars

Turkey Bacon With Scrambled Eggs

Prep Time 25 m | Cooking Time 20 m | 4 Servings

Ingredients:

1/2-pound turkey bacon

4 eggs

1/3 cup milk

2 tablespoons yogurt

1/2 teaspoon sea salt

1 bell pepper, finely chopped

2 green onions, finely chopped

1/2 cup Colby cheese, shredded

Instructions:

1. Place the turkey bacon in the cooking basket.

2. Cook at 360 degrees F for 9 to 11 minutes. Work in batches. Reserve the fried bacon.

3. In a mixing bowl, thoroughly whisk the eggs with milk and yogurt. Add salt, bell

pepper, and green onions.

4. Brush the sides and bottom of the baking pan with the reserved 1 teaspoon of bacon

grease.

5. Pour the egg mixture into the baking pan. Cook at 355 degrees F about 5 minutes.

Top with shredded Colby cheese and cook for 5 to 6 minutes more.

6. Serve the scrambled eggs with the reserved bacon and enjoy!

Per serving:

456 Calories 38.3g Fat 6.3g Carbs 1.4g Protein 4.5g Sugars

CPSIA information can be obtained
at www.ICGtesting.com
Printed in the USA
LVHW061659060421
683575LV00009B/318